Why They Grow Wings

Why They Grow Wings

poems by

Nin Andrews

Silverfish Review Press

Published by Silverfish Review Press
P.O. Box 3541
Eugene, OR 97403

ISBN: 1-878851-15-2

Cover painting *Mosaic Song* © 1996 by Anne Slaughter.
Cover design by Valerie Brewster, Scribe Typography.
Text design by Rodger Moody and Connie Kudura, ProtoType Graphics.

Manufactured in the United States of America.

Acknowledgments

The author wishes to thank the editors of the following magazines in which the poems first appeared:

ACM: "The Silence," "Do Not Ignore This"
American Letters and Commentary: "Making Love to James Dean"
Chelsea: "Been Never Has"
Columbia: "How You Lost Your Red Hat"
Confrontations: "The Life of Borges"
Exquisite Corpse: "Love Stories," "The Christmas Card," "Flying the Friendly Skies"
Gargoyle: "Dedicated to the One I Love"
Green Mountain Review: "The Past"
The Journal: "House Full of Smoke"
Key Satch(el): "A Fairy Tale *Could* Lose Its Pussy,"
Michigan Quarterly Review: "The Dream"
The Paris Review: "Red Blossoms," "The Artichoke," "The Book of Lies"
Ploughshares: "That Cold Summer," "Secondhand Smoke;" "What Is It about the Past"
Poet Lore: "The Afterlife"
Poetry Motel: "First Kiss"
The Prose Poem: "Adolescence," "The Obsession," "Night Fishing"
Salt Hill Review: "Sea World"
Spoon River: "Orange"
Sycamore Review: "Razor Burn"
Virginia Quarterly: "The Truth Further from Nothing," "Living with Cancer"
Yellow Silk: "Selected Orgasms"

"That Cold Summer" was published in *Best American Poetry 1997.*

"What Is It about the Past," was published in the *1995/1996 Anthology of Magazine Verse and Yearbook of American Poetry*, Monitor Book Company, 1997.

"Been Never Has" also appeared in *Voices of Cleveland*, Cleveland State University Press, 1995.

"The Dream" also appeared in *The Female Body*, The University of Michigan Press, 1991.

"Selected Orgasms" also appeared in *The Book of Eros*, Harmony Books, 1995.

"The Arms of Venus," "The Obsession," "Aliens," "Amnesia," and variations on the poems "You" appeared in the chapbook, *Spontaneous Breasts*, Pearl Editions, 1998 (winner of the Pearl chapbook contest).

I would like to thank Stephanie Strickland and Rodger Moody for their advice and careful reading of the text; Denise Duhamel, David Lehman, and Tim Siebles for their inspiration; the faculty of Vermont College, especially Syd Lea and Betsy Sholl; and Beth Gylys for selecting this book.

Special thanks to the Ohio Arts Council for its generous support.

Contents

III FLYING THE FRIENDLY SKIES

This book is dedicated to Jim

I

KANSAS

WHAT IS IT ABOUT THE PAST,

the Old Country where the children we were
walk around in black and white
movies, long nights with bugs
flying in our windows, dreams
slippery as wet fish, moans
in the air from our parents' room? Horses

kicked at their stalls, heat
shivered in the summer skies. Sleepless,
we held our breath, saw shadows
come to life and pulled them inside
us, shutting our eyes. We denied
they existed, denied

we existed, remembering the nuns
at school who wore black to hide
their whiteness, wore black
to show us they were servants
of God. Still, some nights we dream
them, lifting their heavy gowns
as the past unreels, a soundless
movie—a white wall—nobody watching.

ANGELS

By dusk I'd think I saw them,
those ghosts, in the fog
and lifting off the water.
Some nights they were like moonlight
eking into my room.
I don't care what you do,
just leave me be,
I'd want to say
to whatever I thought

was slipping around
in the dark. I'd tighten up
like a cricket in the palm
of a hand, feet and fists
pressing down, afraid to move
even an eyelash. Mornings

I'd squint at the sunlight
on my ceiling,
the polished penny loafers
and plaid kilt on the rocker,
and stare out the window
at a dead leaf
spinning on a strand of web,
at the cow pasture below,
a flurry of sparrows
pecking at cow dung.

Whiffs of bacon
and fried green tomatoes
would glide up the stairwell,
and I'd feel I was coming back,
safe again,

from some place
I'd never admit
I knew.

YOU

Even as a child, I missed you. Often I stared out the window at the dusty hills behind the linens, flapping on the clothesline, beyond the woods where I thought you might live, naming you Franz, Donald, Jim, imagining you were raised by coyotes. Hearing them howl at the moon some nights, I suppressed the urge to howl with them. What if you were an ordinary boy after all, chasing baseballs in your dreams, delivering newspapers at dusk, watching blonde girls with patent leather shoes and silk bows in their hair hanging upside down on the monkey bars? But I knew you would never have endured a past like that, where every human child is a lit baton in an adult's act, existing only to be tossed in the air again and again, hoping to be caught by steady hands.

NIGHT FISHING

We were eating Milk Duds and some
kind of colas on the screen porch,
a moth bopping the light bulb overhead,
me still wearing my itchy wool skirt.

You wanted to take me over the hill
past the barn and show me something.
Like what?
That old rabid dog you keep locked up?

Out back Dad was using the chainsaw
in the dark. Jimmy was chopping wood.
We snuck down to Milton's Pond
where the moon slid on the water.

See that? you asked me.
See what? I asked.
I didn't want any part of you
touching me. Like the moon
was some kind of excuse,
you tore off your clothes

and dove in.
I remember how you looked,
buck naked, belly white,
like a fish jumping,
once he's hooked.

FOXES

Your cigarette tip glows.
You don't say much, just watch
me pull up my black stockings
until the run races up my thigh,

your gaze like sunlight slipping
up my legs. *It's a crazy*
world out there, you laugh,

and I tuck my legs up
underneath me.
We look out the dusty window
where the fox runs past,

a chicken in its mouth.
My chicken, mind you,
and you said you'd kill
that son of a bitch

if I wanted you to.
I want it, bad. *Kill him*,
I say and toss
my ponytail like a blonde

flag. You just pat
my head and smirk, pull out
a jack-knife and clean
your fingernails. *Them foxes*,
you sigh. *They always get away.*

AMNESIA

One summer I spent long hours with therapists. They were puzzled that I could never remember any details about my childhood, and when they fished into my unconscious, trying to loosen the buried memories of a girl, they found nothing but sunlight. One therapist interpreted it to be the light in an operating room. Or the light a person sees after being hit over the head with a brick, or when she dies and comes back to life. I was certain I had never been operated on, nor had I been bopped in the head. That's when I began to tell stories. I told them about angels I had seen turn into stone. I told them I had been adopted at age six by a hard-working couple who milked Jersey heifers for a living, that my first memories were of my tired parents and Madge, a red-haired woman who rented a stall in their cow barn where she boarded Jimbo, a dappled gelding. Madge dressed exclusively in lime green. Cashmere. Madge reminded me of lunar moths I sometimes saw on the naked light bulb at night. Once, when I skinned my knee on the gravel driveway, Madge dismounted Jimbo, picked me up, and hugged me close, pushing me against her huge lime-green bosoms. My lips and cheek brushed her face, and Madge felt smooth and slippery as soap. Nervously I bit into the soft skin around her fingers. When Madge bobbed away again on horseback, rhythmically lifting and lowering her buttocks, her sweatered breasts slow-dancing, I noticed how the eyes of the farm hands and my father slow-danced with them. Even then I knew that bosoms weren't just bosoms. Just as years later I would suspect that orgasms were not merely orgasms. They were tiny messages from the aliens, folded like cloth napkins in a linen drawer.

THE OBSESSION

Occasionally the sailor has visions and sees a woman swimming nude beneath his ship, though, when he dives into the green waves, he finds only white jellyfish, opening and closing like small umbrellas. He remembers the time when he was a boy and imagined ordinary stones such as quartz and fools gold were valuable gems, lovely enough to win the heart of the girl next door. He never bothered to pick the stones up. Even then he knew the girl could never love him. The more he thought about her not liking him, the more he despised her and her adolescent beauty. The more he detested her, the more he wanted to watch her, follow her, sit behind her, and never let her out of his sight. That was the beginning of the obsession.

Evenings he stayed up late, peeking through his Venetian blinds, hoping to catch a glimpse of her in her pink striped pajamas. Every night of the week she would stretch out on the lime carpet in her living room and do her homework in front of the flickering TV. The boy began to believe that if he did not watch her, she might not do her homework. Then she might do poorly in school and be mocked, and he would have to protect her. What if he didn't know how? Better to be certain she did her work.

But the more he stared at her, the more beautiful she became, her skin softening, blushing, and sometimes the touch of her hair on his face wakened him from his dreams. He became convinced his eyes gave off a kind of glow that polished the girl, like an apple, that she could never have been as lovely if he had not looked at her so frequently, so intensely. He thought his staring might have made her breasts grow, just as the sun's heat and light can cause fruit to ripen.

That's when he realized her beauty was a kind of death wish. Like a mirage of an oasis in the Sahara, something that would enhance but never quench his thirst. No wonder years later he still saw her breasts in the middle of the sea. No wonder he hated her.

I SAW AN ANGEL

when I was sixteen. I startled her
in the redbud tree outside
the kitchen window. We exchanged
a long glance. It was the meeting
of two enemies or lovers, I wasn't
sure which, but when I blinked,
she was gone.

I could have seized her
by the throat and held her
captive like a genie,
made her give me her wings.
She'd have had no choice
but to stay here, living my life,
dying my death,

while I flew away. Sometimes
in spring and fall, angels
swoop low and linger
close to the ground. They hover
in doorways and windows, searching.
Sometimes they plummet from the air.
On the way down,

they turn into stones, smooth
white stones you can hold in your hands
and listen to,
hearing the ocean inside you.
Some people think angels that turn
into pebbles are dead

angels. They are wrong. Contrary
to popular belief, angels do not
reach out to men.
They despise them. That's why
they grow wings.

ADOLESCENCE

The winter her body no longer fit, walking felt like swimming in blue jeans and a flannel shirt. Everything stuck to her skin: gum wrappers, Band-aids, leaves. How she envied the other girls, especially the kind who turned into birds. They were the ones boys hand-tamed, training them to eat crumbs from their open palms or to sing on cue. What she would have done for a red crest and a sharp beak, for a little square of blue sky to enter her like wings. But it was her role to sink so the others could rise, hers to sleep so the others could dance. If only her legs weren't too sodden to lift, if only her buttons would unfasten in the water she kept swimming through, and she could extract from the shadow of her breasts a soul as soft as a silk brassiere, beautiful and useless, like a castle at the bottom of the sea.

FIRST KISS

Everything got so still,
I listened to my watch tick
and the quiet of nobody
breathing. Even the hound-
mutt froze, his ears
flat against his head.

I'd been gathering eggs,
slipping them into Dad's
old coat pockets.
A light wind picked up
and whispered something.
A piece of your trousers
fluttered on the barbed wire.

You leaned towards me. I got
a whiff of strong tobacco
and a whole school of minnows
went loose in my blood.

No matter how fast I walked
towards the gate,
I could never get out
of that field.

WHEN DAD LOST IT,

my sister and I'd pretend
he was from Mars. We'd run outside
and hide in the thicket.
Pieces of my pajamas
clung to the cockleburs.
It was a game we played,
being hunted by aliens.
Like a big fish in a sliver
of creek, like a white-tailed deer
in fall, we were easy targets.

Nights I dreamt we were trapped under ice.
All around us I heard the hollow ache
of the winter pond and his screams.
My sister tried to chip me out
with a toothpick.

Mornings after were quiet
as fishermen. We'd wake
to the clock tick and bobwhites,
and tie silk ribbons
in each other's hair.
The sunlight could make everything
as ordinary as toast
and poached eggs. By the time
we drank our milk,
pulled on our knee socks
and saddle shoes and walked to school,
we knew not a solitary thing
ever went wrong in our house.

THE DREAM

I would always wake in a cold sweat, checking the space between my legs to be sure it was still empty.

And when the therapist asked, "Were there disturbing dreams when you were young, the kind that occurred again and again?" I lied, said nothing or claimed my memory was as clean as unlined paper. I thought he knew by the sweat soaking my blouse how

as a child I would dream I was discovered behind the mauve flowered couch at one of my parents' cocktail parties where I liked to hide and listen to Mom and Dad say Lisa was the smartest in her class, Janet, the athlete was the best rider in the state, and I was cross-eyed, though they had hoped to have me fixed.

So far three operations had failed, and you know how important appearance is for a woman. I had been their last hope for a boy, and seemed like one after all, Dad always added. All at once I would be discovered,

naked, hidden, and one guest would announce, "Why congratulations, it's a boy!" I would look down and see it, there between my pale, freckled thighs, a little penis, and all those well-dressed guests, smelling of liquor and perfume and shaving cream

would be touching me with their cold, wet hands, the women's fingernails descending like some rare species of African bird. Men and women would gush and admire the little penis. With so much attention the penis would grow

becoming child size, all on its own, needing to hop, and able to say only one word, "Oh." And you know how penises are, rather friendly fellows, this one being no exception, jumping around in search of good company, personal attention, growing larger by the minute, becoming quite a towering young buck, the kind with a future until my mother, who never liked to hold me, would remark in her crisp, New England accent, "How perfectly grotesque."

The penis would wilt, all at once, ashamed, and hide under the couch, and I would be scolded for hiding behind the couch. Dad would pick me up in his huge, hairy hands, and spank me in front of all those men and women, insisting loudly, "I have to be strict with my girls, to raise them properly in these permissive times."

The guests would withdraw into outer darkness, denying that the penis ever existed. But, night after night, it would rise again.

I wouldn't tell this to anyone for fear of what it might mean.

HOUSE FULL OF SMOKE

Crumpling my notebook paper into a ball, my father asks, *What kind of an idiot are you?* That's me, the idiot girl walking backwards up the stairs with homework I don't understand. All night I hear him, sobering up in the bathroom.

It's a secret underground room with bunk beds and clean sheets, cans of Dinty Moore stew lining the shelves, a hot plate and a tinny radio with extra batteries so everyone can stay tuned to the news about the Russians. Centipedes race up the stone walls. *Someday you'll have to nap down there in the cool darkness,* my father warns. My body is already packed with tiny explosives.

The farm hand tells me when people marry, they mate like the barn cats. Only they call it fucking. He says he's going to buy my sister a red Mustang and drive her away in a cloud of dust. He says he's coming back from Vietnam.

The red fox runs around and around in smaller and smaller circles, blood spattering the snow, a Brueghel painting gone awry. Mounted on the shoulders of the one-armed man, I watch my father raise his rifle and take aim. *Them rabies bit him good,* the one-armed man says. For years after, when I walk alone in the fields, I can hear the fox panting.

Who taught you how to build a Yankee fire? Is that what your mother showed you? My father uncrosses the logs, squeezing them together like proper ladies' legs. *So the flames will lick the wood slow and build up heat. Southern fires, you get blue flame, the hottest brand there is. None of this airy northern stuff.* I watch as the house fills up with smoke.

The snow flies toward the sky, and I lift off the ground and arc back into the saddle. Tears slide up your cheeks and vanish behind my eyes. On my forehead a gash closes, the blood returns to the river beneath my freckled skin. I look so small on top of the chestnut horse, smiling and waving triumphantly at the camera, the sun a halo behind my head. My father holds his hands beneath my foot, offers me a leg down.

ORANGE

A red-haired woman is an ugly woman, my father always said. The year he left, my mother dyed her hair a radiant burnt orange. When I was thirteen, I watched an orange-haired girl. Her name was Sarah. I couldn't speak to her. I stared at her.

After school I saw Sarah by the local pool. She was stretched out on the concrete with no towel. Sweat beaded on her lips. Even the hairs on her belly were orange. Her body was a small meadow of orange.

Sarah, Sarah. Nights I fell asleep, whispering her name, wishing it were my own. For one week we were friends. Every class I sat behind her. Sometimes she brushed her hair until it was comb-lined, strands of hair gliding onto my notebook paper. I braided it, or coiled it around my pencil into a bun before letting it fall.

At the end of the week, Mrs. Repolt, the English teacher, asked us to stay after class. "Girls," she said, "at your age, don't touch other girls."

FEELING IT

I used to watch you
watching me rinse off
at the pump.
I remember once how
the wind parted your hair.
You had a smell to you
I could taste
and Jujubees in your mouth.

Don't you have nothing
better to do? you asked.
Like what, shuck corn?
You slid pennies in my loafers,
took me out for a spin,
then put my hand in your jeans
pocket, saying, *Feel that?*
I pulled out a drill bit
and dropped it on the dash.

That night you took up
flirting with my best friend.
That was the first time
I could feel it
quivering inside me
like a loose blade.

QUICK LICKS

One summer you took up smoking and greasing your hair back.
There were little spots of blood in our chicken eggs.
Fog and black widows clung to my screens. I was
sleepier than I'd ever been. After I washed my hair
with apple-scented cream rinse, bees chased me. One
crawled up inside my dress. I felt like a light bulb
at night. You kept on talking to the air. You said
we wouldn't want to do nothing we'd be ashamed of,
now would we? Your cigarette scorched your fingers.
The garage floor felt cool on my bare knees. I could
smell gasoline and your breath in my dreams. Late
at night we'd ride over to Quick Licks for an ice cream
or a slice of cold custard pie. Sometimes I didn't eat
a thing. Sometimes I made you stop while I stole plums
off the neighbor's tree. I didn't even notice
I was eating them. Everything you wanted to do I did.

II
THE ACCIDENTAL SEDUCTION

THAT COLD SUMMER

At first the angel was perfectly wingless,
loitering in the meadow below our summer place,

gazing up at the sky. A kind of Christina without a home
behind her. Whenever she was hungry, she'd sneak into our house

and steal an apple or a peach from the walnut bowl.
Once she cracked a tooth on a porcelain grape

and bled a milky light, moaning softly
while the white stuff circled her forehead

like a pie plate. You didn't believe it, thinking
she was just another of your crazy imaginings,

not being one to listen much to your own eyes.
Back then you mistook angel blood for a halo.

Approaching her gingerly, you looked at her pale
eyes, afraid to speak, informing me just how airy she was,

like a piece of sky looking at herself. She watched
you like a deer caught in the light, staring

until you touched her shoulder, and she shuddered.
Colder than snow, she was. You said that's why

you invited her in to warm herself. She had a long wind
inside her that fanned the flames

a brilliant blue. Personally, I didn't care for her antics,
but you were enchanted. Had I ever laid eyes

on a thing like that, you'd ask. As if making gales
in my home were a miracle or something. Once I woke

to find her sleeping in the silence beside me, her legs
spread wide as a crooked smile, the white

mist leaking out in a stream. The icy draft
in our bed lasted for weeks. At first

I hardly noticed the feathers slipping into cracks
in the floor, the shopping bags and the soup I kept

simmering on the stove, feathers swimming like dust
in the window light, tiny white feathers with lives

of their own like those brine shrimp they sell
at drug stores to gullible children. Then the feathers

grew more plentiful and blew around the rooms.
I swept them out the door when they rose

and drifted like earthbound clouds. The angel was nowhere
to be seen, though her shadow spread, even grew to tower

over us. Those must have been huge wings sprouting
from her cold shoulders. For me, it couldn't have come

soon enough. Though the house, afterwards, was of a sudden
so familiar and empty, I often wondered how she flew.

A FAIRY TALE *COULD* LOSE ITS PUSSY,

I reasoned after you left. Thus there was once a princess, who, perhaps like most princesses had no idea she had a magic pussy (or was it a bird, a star, a tulip, a mere figment? She didn't know for sure, nor do I). Not in the early days, not when she married her first prince and wanted nothing to do with him. In bed, that is (where else?). It was her pussy (or maybe her swan, bell, petunia) who disliked the prince. A lot can be learned from a reasonable pussy (phoenix? Or is it God?) since it's the pussies that know the language of the future and all the songs of the spinning world. The prince was often jealous of her (and her pussy, her soft-spoken sparrow, her little begonia) and wanted to know of whom she dreamt and for whom she was keeping her pussy (her mourning dove). Having never thought much of her pussy (and related winged things), and why she kept its small doorway (from whence came such sounds: soft humming, occasional wolf howls) carefully away from him, she, too, began to wonder. The more jealous he grew, the more wild (exotic) her pussy grew, until it opened its soul wider and wider, and her dreams were not her own but were the dreams of her (plumed) pussy. Like flowers in a warm meadow, the pussy became so frisky and lush, so frolicsome and heavenly that one day it simply flew off (or blew off on its glistening feathers, or did it depart in its private UFO, with the darkest angels), far from her small, silent body. Without her pussy (chariot), the princess had no dreams at all, no reason to live (sigh, breathe). And so she languished while her pussy (spirit) wandered across foreign lands and lovers. Like an immigrant, an outsider to her own body and dreams, the pussy (cloud) drifted happily forever after. Yes, there was, even then, such a thing as happily ever after. And a winged pussy. Once upon a time.

THE AFTERLIFE

No getting around it. To truly love
the man of your dreams,
you must become a dream. Never mind
that he's already given you
his first-born son, his last name,
and twenty-six recipes for instant bliss. Never mind
that he's made your skeleton into a piano,
soft music from your bones.
It's not enough. A woman knows these things
and the dark taste of smoke on your lips.
Women understand the term, love at first sight,
those wingless girls, riding escalators
up and down, expecting a chariot
to descend from the clouds. So go ahead.
Send him that special photo of yourself, the one
that makes you fade into someone else. Sooner
or later he'll catch a glimpse
of your red scarf, vanishing behind a building.
Or your mink hat as you're slipping into a yellow cab,
the very one he's been waiting for
after all these years.
How slowly your edges will soften.
Until one day you can touch him,
only with your breath.
You will be released into his thoughts.
You who are so delicious, wispy.
He'll adore you as a figment. Studying you
as a rare species of animal,
he'll stop and see, wincing ever so slightly
as he runs his pale fingers
through his hair. Then, like the blue
fading from the sky at night,

you will enter a world behind the world,
not of cocks, but of the souls of cocks,
and their terrible grief.
Your breasts will come alive in the palm
of his hands. It will happen as naturally
as water rising through a stalk,
breaking you apart. Or into bloom.

RED BLOSSOMS

The uncanny ability, an instinctual dance, a mind on safari, the scent of blossoms, the foraging flight, the uncanny ability, to cling, to find, to fly into a mind on safari, the scent of blossoms, feet as small as eyelashes, slipping in, an instinctual dance, a sign language, circling, slowly, crawling deeper, feet as small as eyelashes, into the tulip's center, a sign language, folding his wings, combing the surface with his tongue, crawling deeper into the tulip's center, spiraling down, folding his wings, combing the surface, the sugary juices, the warm petals, wind rustling leaves and ladies' dresses, spiraling down, pollen stuck to skin, hair, his wings, the sugars and juices of warm petals, rustling leaves and ladies' dresses, clutching the inner parts of the blossom, pollen stuck to legs, hair, wings, to the sweetness all over his fur, clutching the inner parts of the blossom, drunk with nectar, heavy, the sweetness all over his fur, the delirious silk of red blossoms, drunk with nectar, heavy, lifting up the delirious silk of red blossoms.

LOVE STORIES

The writing assignment was to find out which animal or plant you identified with, and write from that perspective. According to the teacher, there is a mysterious kinship between man, plant, and animal. For example, he asked, do you prowl, slink, or slither? Do you enjoy the excitement of the hunt? Or do you sit so still, an undetected morsel in camouflage? Are you coveted for your silky, pink petals, your tasty meat, or your startling yellow wings?

The woman at the checkout counter told me getting married was a lot different from living at home. After the wedding and the honeymoon, she had to make a lot of choices, like the one between a sack of red-skinned potatoes and a blouse. Did I know what she meant? I was purchasing several sacks of peanuts, still in the shell.

Boris, the lyric poet, told me that no obstacle would slow the revolution, taking place in his soul, the ballet of the nude angel. He said the soul is always female, and he meets his soul in the bodies of nudes. Lately he's been seeing his soul in Mary's body, the one in his mind, not the one beneath her clothes.

Roger wrote a poem about Mary's dark center where heaven and earth (or is it heaven and hell?) met. I told him it was sexist to write about a woman like that. He stared at me blankly and explained that Mary was a mollusk in his animal exercise.

Mary's best kept secret is millet, a tiny yellow cereal sold at gourmet stores which ranks high in iron and protein and is thought to have the secret ingredient of aphrodisia, unquenchable sexual thirst. Millet, when properly prepared, has a lofty, nutty flavor. Mary said Boris prefers grits.

Late into the night I watched videos, feeling on my skin the tiny sparks flying between the hero and heroine. A lunar moth stretched its pale green wings against my screen. When I woke up, you were gone.

THE ARTICHOKE

What an ugly specimen. The first time I saw it, I thought of Grandma's bathing cap, green and shrunken after all these years. I sliced it open, tasted the pale flesh, until gradually she offered herself up, leaf by leaf. In her depths she held a tiny, faded star, a spark that fell in a meteor shower over Frank's garden. Slowly I developed a taste for her expensive style: fancy restaurants, candlelit wines. Sometimes we stayed in and read by the fire, drinking the leftover melted butter, wiping the grease on our shirt sleeves. I introduced her to friends. Each of them adored her, said she was irresistible. She had the heart of a Buddha. Green leaves of flame. Nightly I grasped her like a seashell and listened to the nothing philosophers spend lifetimes writing about. Slowly she acquired the chilled look of a vegetable, kept in the icebox all day. Then one evening there were no leftovers. I went to the grocery store. The sales clerk said artichokes are out of season. This is not San Diego. Still I dreamt of her, dipped in lemony butter, scraped clean with the teeth and sucked, the pale cream of flesh, the tender flower, her skirt held up like a cup, each sip pulling me closer to the moon, the vegetable pearl of her insides where the heart fans out fibrous hairs and waits a last mouthful of her green world.

MAKING LOVE TO JAMES DEAN

The man I love more than anyone else in the world married someone else. I could have married someone else. He would have married me then, but I would have refused on principle. Why would I want to marry someone who wants to marry someone else? He married a beautiful blonde, a babe far younger than I. I'm not a bit jealous, though, because I know a man can be impressed with soft skin, big breasts, and pearly white teeth only so long

before he loses interest in the body and thinks only of the divine. The man I didn't marry thinks sex is sacred. So he saves it up. Only Sundays are holy. On no other day of the week does he think about sex. Did you know the average human thinks of sex every six seconds? I read that fact in *The Art of Ecstasy.* Or was it *The Ecstasy of Art?* Monday through Saturday the man I didn't marry thinks about not thinking about sex. Sometimes, when the man I didn't marry is making love, he thinks about making love so hard, he has an out of the body experience. He looks down at me from the ceiling and shimmers like a candle in the wind. He feels as helpless as a flame about to be snuffed out as he hovers there, above the body's surges. It's a bit like making love with an empty mirror, he says matter-of-factly, and I wonder, am I the empty mirror?

Or is he? Drifting and observing like an audience from another world leaves so much to be desired. And I do. I desire it, all. Whatever *it* is, he used to sigh. As if sex, or his cock, were the ultimate mystery. And what is truth or sex, if not something in the mind, or on it? Or out of it? He would ask, talking on and on as if it wasn't him I made love to, after all. Whenever I shut my eyes, he'd ask, who are you seeing beneath those lids? As if he suspected it was someone else, and so was I. As if he knew it wasn't I who made love to him on our Sunday matinees. It was Natalie Wood. I couldn't tell him that James Dean never could get enough of Natalie's pale skin, no matter what day of the week it was. What we needed was a vacation, I often suggested,

imagining us moving to a cave some place in the mountains, hanging out in the dark until the man I didn't marry couldn't tell Sunday from Wednesday, until every day of the week was sacred. After all, Sunday is just an idea, not a day at all. Like James Dean, like sex. It could happen at any hour sexy enough to stay in bed with the man I love, or would love to love. Or whom I imagine I might love to love. But who would that be, he asked, again and again,

wanting to know. Then I'd picture all the men I'd ever loved lifting off my flesh like moths from a light bulb when you cut the switch. In the end there was only James Dean, clinging faithfully to my skin.

SECONDHAND SMOKE

One day, even the geography shifted.
Overnight our seaside resort became winter dark
in Detroit. Tall buildings stared me down
at dusk, and like rush hour denizens
pressed their gray bodies into mine. Like me
they were all insomniacs. Their shadows
quivered in coffee cups, tasting of secondhand smoke.
One corporate center whispered it had always wanted
to open its windows, empty its offices
and corridors of paper and plastic furniture,
just lift off, the wind blowing
through its hollow stairwells. Were it to open
one window at a time, you would hear its soul
like a flute or maybe a clarinet.
The funeral parlor on Sixth Street was afraid
of heights. It had dreams of sailing away
with the cathedral at Chartres. Always in love
with Gothic sorts, especially those bedecked
with gargoyles, I imagined sinking slowly,
watching the fish enter the chapel,
feeling the pulse of warm waves and sand at my feet.
There are spaces in things and spaces between
that hold the color of sorrow,
the soundless movies no one watches, playing
and playing on our walls. Better than anyone,
these listless structures understood the strain
of memories, his footsteps on their frigid tile.
And how I could not follow,
and they held me there in their yellow light.

THE TRUTH FURTHER FROM NOTHING

It's your absence I fell in love with. The body
behind the body, the dream within the dream,
behind the borders of the photograph where you left
a jet stream on the rumpled silk sky, where each shoe
walked away with a breast, and leaving was a way
of life. Sometimes we abandoned our own skin,
the musty corridors of memory, husks of childhood,
choirs of dead bees on the sills. On the floor
Mother's hand-me-down slip became the southern haze
I grew up inside. No one lives there now. Or here
where I dream I'm as small as a sweet potato,
resting in the slope between your rib cage
and hip bones. Too leaden to lift, your limbs
tell me what I often forget. The truth is nothing
I believe. The nothing that holds your caress
and permanent address. Like your teeth in my thighs.
Like the nights that fly around the room several times
before bursting into flames, your wingtips
pacing the empty rooms inside me, your freckled
hands, frequent guests to my skin, and my clinging,
a frantic moth, beating against your screen.
Like the shape of an hour or our body when one
passes into another. And the aftermath when trees
take long walks inside us, and no one hears us fall.

THE ARMS OF VENUS

You'd have been proud of me, Love. I took a trip alone to the art museum. I didn't simply visit with Mabel and eat spinach salad, picking out the bacon bits and egg yolks. A traveling exhibit of Greek sculptures brought busloads of visitors, and I kept staring at a lovely male statue with a chipped place where the penis once was. The other day I read a note posted on the glass door of The Pasta Palace, *Cook Needed.* I was sure it said *Cock Needed.* Didn't you tell me the Greek artisans sculpted idealized versions of men and women and painted them in exquisite colors? Of course all the color is gone. Which reminds me of our discussion of Venus de Milo's arms. You said it makes no difference that she's armless. But she looks so defenseless without them. I can't help picturing her lovely white arms, how they must be deep in the soil of history, reaching up or down in a gesture of despair. Once they hung from her stone body, one arm covering her breasts, one hand demurely shielding her crotch like a fig leaf. It's the missing parts, Love. They matter. What they add. What they take away.

SEA WORLD

At last I understand my problem. And after all these years. I have been meditating incorrectly. I have been chanting *Om* to calm the vast ocean of my mind. Only men who wish to leave the world of lust and lawn mowers forever can say *Om* in peace. *Om*, I only just discovered, lacks the sumptuous sounds and multi-syllabic soft centers appropriate for females of my specific social class. A blonde, freckled woman from Suburban, Ohio must never say *Om*. The Maharishi Mahesh Yogi, his holiness himself, phoned me from New Delhi to express his sincerest concerns for my health. *Om*, he sighed, can never be kept awash with light. In Himalayan caves male devotees chant *Om* until they levitate and hover upside down like bats. They breathe only through their left nostrils, and in their spare time, they balance cinder blocks on their cocks. Such performances are said to be reminiscent of the seal acts at Sea World in Aurora, Ohio.

Alas. What happens to the women of *Om*? Women whose perfect silence is unpetaled by a tiny scrap of sound?

Woe is me. For too many days, *Om* is all I have known. *Om* is all I can think. Already my breasts are rising like the heads of seals beneath my blouse and growing stiff with excitement.

HOW I GREW WINGS

After you left me, I had two revelations. The first: I become someone else with each act of making love. Whom I can never remember. It is a kind of haphazard evolution, like falling to the ground after flying. Or is it rising? Not that I let on that I can fly, not to just anyone. It takes a while to climb inside the air, inhabit it, and glide. Afterwards it's difficult to inhale, to put my feet on the ground and walk, one step at a time, to remember who or how it was I am. And whom I just made love to. That was my second revelation. I never made love to you when we made love. Not even once.

III

FLYING THE FRIENDLY SKIES

RAZOR BURN

I believe in the radio, cannot properly drive unless the speakers are throbbing. *The way to live your life is with death on your shoulder,* says a crackling baritone on the radio. I live with death on my shoulder when I drive my white van. *Imagine you can fly like a bird.* That's what the rishi on the car radio says this morning. I always think I can fly. A rishi is a great teacher, and the rishi says each of us has a rishi inside us. My daughter, Sue, is late for school. I'm speeding past a truck carrying lawn mowers, almost crashing into a speeding red MG, honking at some asshole in the MG. I flip him the bird and, thinking about cops and death and rishis, speed up. The rishi says if you live with death on your shoulder, you can get anything you want. You can do anything you want, too, even walk through fire and never burn. Sue is terrified of fire. But she isn't listening yet. Instead she's telling me that Stephanie Combs has her own Visa card and eats at restaurants every evening. If we go to a restaurant, Sue has to blow the candle out in the middle of the table. Sometimes the waitress tries to light the candle again, but Sue gets hysterical when the match descends. *Picture your life as a flame and live in the heat of the moment,* the rishi continues. *Then walk through the fire without, and the flames will feel as cool as waves crashing over your toes on a sandy beach in South Carolina.* Who is this raving lunatic, Sue wants to know. Someone should lock him up. I tell her that the radio-rishi is what we all have locked up inside us. A crazy fire-walker who never burns or sleeps, just talks. That's how we live. I imagine my daughter strolling eagerly into a blaze, with naked legs and arms, and emerging unsinged. The fire might free me once and for all from my fears that are slow-dancing every evening when I watch her get in the car with Jeremy Crothers. Once you are free of fears, you can live as a rishi on a radio, I think aloud. Sue is waving out the window at Jeremy Crothers. He acts as if he doesn't see her, and when we stop the van, she checks for pimples in the rear-view mirror, sighs and says, *Listen, Mom—*

whatever you do, don't talk about radio-rishis in front of Jeremy, okay? I wave at her and listen to the rishi describe how some less evolved people, the kind with incorrect beliefs, burn like paper. They can be reduced to ashes at the slightest touch. I pull away. Leave them embracing below clouds the color of ashes. I can't help seeing my daughter reduced to ashes and air at the slightest touch of Jeremy Crothers.

THE SILENCE

As an adolescent I imagined I could vanish. First my hands would become transparent. Then my arms would follow, and my torso, until I was nothing and could walk through walls and trees and strangers. I visited entire cities of silent streets and invisible women. Their words escaped them. Their bodies felt as unfamiliar as a second language.

Daily I practiced invisibility. Silent and indistinct as a shadow, I watched myself from afar, drifting like a thought, having long ago shed the skin and voice of a blonde, freckled girl others saw and knew, her need to surrender to mirrors and lovers, to curl up in a dreamless sleep, allowing hands and a long ribbon of hours to glide over her.

Nights, when I fall asleep in your arms, I dream I'm standing on the lime shag carpet of my childhood, sneaking crustless cucumber sandwiches from a cocktail tray. I'm always naked. Circling me, smiling adults admire the body of a child I once was, closing their fingers over my knees like cats' paws.

After the last of my child was sucked out, the doctors said I shouldn't feel guilty. Usually babies who aren't quite right slip out early. It's nature's way. I felt nothing. For weeks I slept in the city of invisible women who walk on sock feet. Their bodies rose like smoke in the morning light I stared through. Together we watched my child sinking in the clear blue of a chlorinated pool by The Golden Hours, that roadside motel where we honeymooned in another life.

LIVING WITH CANCER

Who says there is no healing? Just the other morning
my cousin showed me her saline breasts. In a matter of weeks
the nipples will be tattooed on. Size double C, she smirks.
Just like my adolescent dream. So it doesn't hurt
when the body screams, she becomes a body without a mind,
a mind without a body. Like a letter without an envelope,
an envelope with no message inside. That's how I see
life, she says. Sometimes, her breasts have phantom
pains. And leak imaginary milk when the baby cries.

After chemo, she forgets whose baby it is. And whose body
she's in. Her lips travel the air as wings. We feel them
kiss us like dry stalks or leaves. Nights I imagine her
hovering in the doorway, though it's only the dreams
gliding everywhere. Like strands of hair, they come loose

at the source. While the surgeon's hands move behind her skin,
we wait, reading the manual of new age miracles, a dying man's
last vision seen by x-ray, a one-way window through which
the dead look back and see only a child's ballet. At last
we are ushered from the waiting room to join the other members
of the blonde family running across the cover of the slick
magazine, *Living with Cancer*. We, too, could be endlessly
racing on a green meadow without a drop of sky I.V.-ed in.

THE PAST

You had to be young to get in. Every time
I describe it, it's not the same
place. The cargo of radio tunes and sorrow
comes loose like strands of Mother's hair
from a bun. The scent of her lemon
perfume and lilac skin cream, her caress,

that summer night we went crabbing together,
leaning over the pier's edge, casting off
lumps of bait, watching

by flashlight the eerie loping sideways gait
of our prey. Mother kept describing
the music of Bach as the sound of little boxes
and numbers and hours,
like a crab-walk gliding over the piano keys.

Mozart was miles of water, so much
it hurt to be held down
by the waves. While listening to Mozart,

she said, Granddaddy researched the salt
and water balance of the body, inventing
the IV. He worked late, his lamp always lit . . .

I remember our net of crabs,
the cold, bright enclosures of light
like the screened in porch where my father
rocks, combing his gray hair and humming.

How long he lives past his wishes. His gaze,
a world inside water we can't see
into. He slides toward senility slowly. Sundays

we visit him dutifully, walking home along the blind
shoulders of highways, expecting
a lift from some benevolent stranger. Silhouettes
is all we are. Lit from behind.

THE CHRISTMAS CARD

Dear ________,

As we now embrace the holiday season, I cannot help savoring the sweetness of memories of summer and friends that flood my very heart and mind. Oh for summer, the season when tender zephyrs do caress my skin! When one flits about like a destiny-bound butterfly!

Here in Shaker Heights, I still live with my husband, Jud, and our two lovely children, Beatrice and Bobo. For those of you who have not had the pleasure of meeting Jud, Jud has searing blue eyes, unswerving loyalty, a facility for accruing wealth, and a fine, freckled rosy complexion. Beatrice, a second-grader (already! I can hardly believe it myself), displays a dazzling talent as a budding ballerina and is an avid reader who passes many hours in pursuit of books. Beatrice has already read *The Iliad, The Odyssey* and *Finnegans Wake.* Bobo, our first-grader, follows in Jud's footsteps, exhibiting a nimble wit, endearing charms, and a vast capacity for watching Sunday afternoon football and Arnold Schwarzenegger. Bobo, who has always manifested a dramatic flair, will be Maid Marian's father in the school play of Robin Hood, a part he plays swimmingly.

Though there is many a thistle upon the silken rose plants of parenthood, I remain convinced that the key to successful parenting lies within the management of daily minutiae. I couldn't agree more with Barbara Bush who says that in the end of her life, a woman will not value her career. Still, I take ample time to think about other people and world conditions, and thus I busy myself with the Junior Committee. Indeed I fancy myself a humanitarian and stick my fingers in many pies. And how often I praise the heavens above for giving me Jud who is simply bristling with health and vibrancy and recent personal growth. Ever-faithful, Jud continues to seek God in airport chapels whenever he travels.

How the year has fled! May the seasonal blessing be upon you! Like a windowbox atumble with flowers, may you be atumble with joy this Christmas season! How often we think of you, __________, our most beloved of friends!

Yours truly,

Jud, Barb, Beatrice and Bobo

DO NOT IGNORE THIS

This pussy has been sent to you. This pussy has been around the world seven times. You will receive luck within six days of receiving this pussy. You will forget all suffering. But always you must remember one thing, the pussy. Alexander Diaz received this pussy in 1953. Where is this pussy from? he asked his secretary. But she didn't recognize it. A few days later, his office worker, Constantine Collins, found the pussy and took her home where, alas, after a single luscious dusk, he promptly abandoned her. This is no joke. Both Augustine Diaz and his office worker languished. While crossing Main Street, they were flattened by a speeding bulldozer. Divine punishment. Please be forewarned. This pussy has toured the world. She has opened like a parachute and sailed from flaming planes. She has manifested plagues of locusts in paradise. This pussy can bring palpitations and perils. Sometimes men look so small to the pussy (pardon her manners), she swallows them whole. But men, she notes, they linger. They are little more than spice on her breath. It's true, my friend. You must not overlook the truth. This pussy was sent to you. She is empty now. As empty as a sidewalk in Cyprus at 3:00 a.m. on a Sunday morning. Faith has no price. She must never be set aside. Denis de Rhodes received her in 1973. He, too, left her alone while swimming in the ocean. She slipped his mind and floated like a jellyfish to distant shores. Denis's children, Donna and Pete, were never allowed a recess. His wife, poor Madame de Rhodes, who knew nothing of the pussy, beseeched her spouse for help and advice before noticing that he had dried up in his sleep. Poetic justice. For three years the de Rhodes lived on seaweed and snails in a cave on the beach. They grew hair all over their limbs and torsos and vanished with a wandering tribe of lusty sea apes. This pussy speaks with few words. She can tell each insect wing from the wind and every shred of cloud from the bypassing horizons. She is in love with celestial things and inhuman deeds. She can devour the pit of any man, no matter if it's true that he is the rottenest little plum. Faith has no half-life. Nevertheless, the pussy feels alone in the rain and Laundromats, there where Robert Diaz, grandson of Alexander, left her one leaf-blown dusk in late August. Robert still dwells in the abyss as a shadow of a shadow of a shadow of himself. Or of the one who left all his clothes and the pussy on eternal spin. The constable found him naked and babbling in the gutter on some island off the coast of Japan, his cock bobbing like a conductor's baton. The pussy fears that you, too, will leave her behind. Perhaps you already have. You have forgotten her for reasons all your own. You who were once as happy as a beetle in the sun. Or as a crooning tree frog after the deluge. As an ant atop a sticky bun. Can you spare a few crumbs? Tonight the moon is almost full. Listen to the stars roaming the streets. Enchanted by the moon, they will always sleepwalk while humming softly. As you did, once, my love, yes, once upon a time, upon a pussy. Tell me, are you dreaming of her much? Of the future? The pussy? I fear not. As always the pussy will have no choice. Too soon she will be erasing you from the face of the earth and outer space. Alas. She had hoped for so much more from you than the rest. This could be your last chance. Though I admit, it might be too late.

SELECTED ORGASMS

The Orgasm's First Date:

On their first date, Franz asked Maria, when was the first time you had an orgasm? Maria stared back with the wan look of orgasm starvation.

The Hypothetical Orgasm:

Franz looked at the orgasm from afar. Maria thought about it. The two analyzed it, as if it were a hypothesis. All at once, they were seized by the orgasm. For a moment they looked back at the world as one would look at a hypothetical world.

Cezanne's Orgasm:

Beneath the brush strokes the orgasm becomes peaches and pears. Such golden reds and oranges.

Van Gogh's Orgasm:

The orgasm flies through the air, its hair flaming out across the night.

Pollock's Orgasm:

Maria sighed, if only he'd learn a little self control...

Picasso's Orgasm:

She knew what he was thinking. How he'd like to strip off her white skirt and silk blouse and panties and take her apart piece by piece. See how she worked. And leave her spread all over the floor.

De Kooning's Orgasm:

It seemed to rise into the room without them.

Cezanne's Second Orgasm:

Sometimes the orgasm dreams it's a peach. It basks in the sun and the summer rain. And ripens in its own sweet time.

Picasso's Second Orgasm:

The orgasm split Maria in half. Franz never did find all her missing parts or her lace panties, though yesterday he discovered her left breast on the sitting room table.

De Kooning's Second Orgasm:

When the orgasm is not part of the man, the woman, and the dream, it cools. Then they call it an abstract orgasm.

Inside the Orgasm:

Inside the orgasm there were no windows, soft waves or sunlit sheets, no gods or memories. Inside the orgasm were Franz and Maria who were no longer Franz and Maria.

Aerial Orgasms:

When the angels first saw Franz and Maria, they were delighted. Franz and Maria were the new kids on the block. The angels wanted someone else to fly with, but what a disappointment the humans were, always sinking like stones. Still, they enjoyed a little taste of the sky, even if they could stand it, only for a moment.

Monogamous Orgasms:

Maria was one woman with three orgasms. In each orgasm she was another woman. In each orgasm she saw another man, though she slept with only one man.

The Absent Orgasm:

Franz and Maria don't have to be in every panel. Sometimes orgasms take place without them.

The Silent Orgasm:

The silent orgasm stared back at Franz, waiting for translation. But who can translate silence?

The Frigid Orgasm:

Today she is a stone. The orgasm is a cloud imprisoned in her stone flesh.

The Lousy Orgasm:

Afterwards they ate calamari that tasted like tiny tires.

The Zen of the Orgasm:

One must enjoy leaving the orgasm as much as entering it. That is the way of the enlightened.

The Orgasm's Mantra:

The orgasm is always whispering one word in Franz and Maria's ears: "Goodbye."

DEDICATED TO THE ONE I LOVE

It's simply hopeless, isn't it? Even if you begin
by postulating the existence of some exotic place—
a village of divine origin, or diabolical perhaps—
maybe a city of sin, or hindrances such as torpor and lust
(those are the ones I like best), whole days spent in bed,
wearing silk pajamas, sipping cappuccino, daydreaming—
going backwards in time (you could visit Paris in the first
half of the century if you wish), gliding down banisters
and into the ballrooms of the past where, by some odd chance,
you already know the steps to all the dances, you, Darling,
would still become a politician, some charismatic figure
issuing proclamations at every hour. And no matter what you say
or said, it would create the illusion of making sense, inspiring
    shock,
warning of imminent and supreme crisis without end—and all
    at once
we'd be back in the dark ages, and then the desert—
and you would decide to leave (don't you always?), slipping on
your coat and glasses (alas) and rushing off before the part begins
with Jacob wrestling the angels, and all the patriarchs go limp—

but you wouldn't resist gazing back (would you? just once?)
through the promised lens—to see me again, there where I am
forever lazing in bed, combing my long blonde hair over my
    shoulders
and nude breasts? Outside the sky is shimmering, and it's dusk
in Jerusalem (or is it Valencia or Madrid?), and someone is ringing
the doorbell again and again, and I am imagining God is as happy
with the world (unredeemed as it is) as an ant atop a wet, bruised
    peach.

HOW YOU LOST YOUR RED HAT

One night Houdini says to me, Honey, I'm sorry.
You can't love the same woman twice. I should never
have come back. I need to put on my hat and vanish
like an absent mind. Houdini had a red hat
he never wore until that night, though he often said
to me, the soul is nothing but a hat balanced loosely
on your blonde hair. Take it off if you want.
Times like this, his body is all
I want. Houdini levitated into the city sky.
And my soul with him, a bowler hat spinning
slowly down until I was caught beneath it
on top of another man's bald head.

MY APHRODISIAC

I want to tell you one thing:
you are wrong.
About everything.

Consider perspective as a case in point.
You loved to inform me
that far-away things appear smaller.

I want to inform you
that distant things grow bigger.
Missing objects are the largest of all.
Their shadows can loom above us
and darken an entire universe.
In a single instant, they build cities
of memory without a misplaced word.

I know this for a fact.
At a certain point in a life,
an absence begins to grow. Your shadow,
for example, is now drifting across my sheets
and ceilings. Just the other night,
you were standing behind me
in the mirror and in the department store
windows and on the subway and at Arabica's
coffee shop, and when I stared at my eyes
to apply mascara, I glimpsed you
in the dark glow of my pupils. In desperation,
I called to a man walking beneath my window,
and he became you, answering my call
with a grin, opening the door to my apartment

with his sleeves rolled up to his elbows,
his cold smoker's fingers. Instantly
I caught a whiff of his fragrance,
inhaled him as deeply as a summer rose.
Such a scent! Call it bliss, eternity,
oblivion, seventh heaven, the names
of a thousand and one perfumes, the scent
of a man in heat. Oh yes, men are in heat.
Everywhere. Now that you are gone.

BEEN NEVER HAS

All for once I melt to like it, even now
you're everywhere I see. Part-crazy
that is. My city, too, and turn whenever
I do on personal nothing street, kiss cold, winding
bliss, snatches of wail and moan, want
doesn't who? Been never has, there but, head my lay
up curl to want your body glow, but you're all
hollow, darling. Isn't it the same the isn't
is but? Laid or drunk with up living you, Cleveland.

THE BOOK OF LIES

It's true. I lied. Isn't that how
we stay alive? Dr. Metz in Old Testament
101 said Moses parted the reeds on a lake
not the Red Sea. The orgasm was a fake
like the waves of applause and the wing beats
of one hundred birds lifting from our hearts.
Give me a break. You call this love?
Outside the sky is white, not blue, and the only
person who calls me is from Purple Heart.
Have you any spare parts to give away? I do,
I do. The sign says cook needed, not cock
wanted. And when I said I love you, I meant,
Get lost, Asshole. The man with red hair
and green eyes cleaned me out of orgasms long ago,
and silk underpants too. He left for Chattanooga
in a red Camaro with six boxes of All Bran
and a blonde bimbo so gorgeous she made me cry.
The archangels never blew their trumpets.
Silence is the music of the spheres
and the messiah's dark scream. The witch ate Hansel,
and Gretel, too. I live in a chocolate house
in Berlin. The red-haired man was never here.
When they tore down the wall, he left
with a suitcase full of bricks and my twin.
Her name was Faith. I never knew his.

THE LIFE OF BORGES

The Borgesian sex life, the logic of minimal coitus and the womanless man is really quite simple. One lady fixed him for life. Once Borges slept with a prostitute, and the orgasm brought him so close to death, he feared it forever after. No one knows how she did it for sure. Perhaps she was an impenetrable mystery. A genuine ravaging sexual Pasiphae, an insatiable woman who lusted after white bulls. Maybe in the library of Babel, you can find her photo, writhing dangerously there between the pages and amidst descriptions of the various sources and of male unsexuality. In any case, Borges loved his mother too much. Everyone knows a man who loves his mother can never fully enjoy women.

The biographer of Borges dreamt of Borges, alive and warm, but not throbbing. He could not picture Borges, his own Borges, a man with unbridled imagination, loose on the body of a live woman. He knew that there was a reason, a terrible hidden secret.

Enter the prostitute. Of course, nobody saw her, and surely no one knew what Borges did with her. The reader of the biography of Borges does not need to follow the threads of his imagination into the locked room of Borges and the prostitute. Sparing us any unnecessary speculations, the biographer concludes: the orgasm almost destroyed our renowned Argentinian.

A Borges biographer understands such matters. He knows a man could be hurt for a lifetime after one night in bed with the wrong sort of woman. Of course, no one saw the biographer in bed with such a lady. Afterwards he might have told tales of a terrifying sexual episode, concluding with a volcanic climax, an eruption of dynamic proportions that shook the very center of his being while the woman lay calm and unmoved. Such occurrences could limit the future of even the healthiest young blade. I know. I shall restrain myself from exhaustive explanations. It is I alone who understands the biographer of Borges.

FLYING THE FRIENDLY SKIES

Lately I've been spending my days alone, staring into the blue air above, flying the friendly skies. A singular experience always beginning with a mere memory, a little twinge, an ache, and suddenly I was lifting towards the heavens like a helium balloon and directly into the arms of an unknown lover. I gradually became accustomed to rising in the air at any moment, trusting the sky beneath me, the empty spaces in mind and body. Miraculously, no one could detect my frequent flights, and I learned to continue the normal affairs of daily life as if nothing unusual were occurring.

Now, as long as there is a blue sky overhead, even a walk down the sidewalk on an ordinary day can trigger unexpected surges of pleasure. I frequently sigh over flowers, neighbors' dogs, babies, and bushes. Sometimes I can only sigh and gasp, "What a gorgeous day!"

When people are amazed by my exuberance, I explain that I am a poet. I gush over their lovely silver hair, their dewy eyes, their moist lips, the little freckles on their noses. I gaze into their faces with such adoration. Sometimes, I admit, I pant a little. Or frolic in the autumn mist. I can barely survive the intoxication of such moments. Without hesitation, people excuse themselves from my presence.

Now, at last, I spend my days in solitary bliss.

WINGS

One day the cold entered me. I had to fold my wings around me and shiver for warmth. Cutting the flesh like baby teeth, the wings, still new, fluttered all night in front of the oscillating fan and cast us always in a collage of shadows. There was no longer enough room in the bed, so I slept on my feet in the den, cursing the awful weight of feathers. Until I grew strong enough to keep them aloft, they would drag in the dirt, sweeping rainwater and stones across our oak floors. Like a stray dog I smelled of rotting leaves but would no longer stand for soaps or perfumes. Gradually I grew attached to the wings, and even practiced rising and falling through the mist which was a soft place, but with the chilled sorrow of a fugue. Leaping first from chairs, then rooftops, I hardly noticed when we stopped speaking to one another. When I wasn't learning how to soar, I enjoyed a restless sleep, and celestial music droned in my dreams, piercing my nerves like a radio alert. One day I'd had enough. Drifting further and further from the coast, I flew off. Strangers watched me leave. I know how we promised to keep our secrets to ourselves, but the halo slid slowly down of its own accord, like a drop from a faucet. That's what always happens. At first resistance, clinging to the impossible. Then, without saying goodbye, she was gone.